To: Gloria

Our Blood Remembers

poems by

Lois Red Elk

Many Voices Press
Flathead Valley Community College

Cover Design by Sally Johnson

Special Thanks to Hannah Bissell and Amy Jaeger

Many Voices Press is a non-profit press from Flathead Valley Community College. Donations are tax deductible. We depend on the generosity of people like you. For more information on our books, please contact:

Lowell Jaeger, Editor
Many Voices Press
Flathead Valley Community College
777 Grandview Drive
Kalispell, Montana 59901

Phone: (406) 756-3907
Web Address: manyvoicespress.fvcc.edu
Email: ljaeger@fvcc.edu

Softbound ISBN — 0983367906
ISBN — 9780983367901

Cataloging-in-Publication data on file at the Library of Congress.
Library of Congress Control Number: 2011923050

Created, produced, and designed in the United States.
Printed in the United States.

Cover Artist: Dustin Noble Red Elk Reed is an enrolled member of the Fort Peck Sioux of Montana. He was five years old when he began drawing and has always been encouraged by his tiospaye (family) to pursue his art. He especially admires the work of his grand-uncle Herman Red Elk (a well-known hide painter) and the cultural arts of his aunts. In 1990 he studied at the Institute of American Indian Arts. A working artist, he is an illustrator, a creator of three-dimensional Sioux art implements, and an innovator in mixed media. The cover image of ***Our Blood Remembers*** is titled "Gifts from the Tipi." He is the son of Lois Red Elk and Dennis Reed.

Dustin writes: "In Sioux culture the tipi is owned by the woman. It also represents the family; the poles are the man and children, and the covering is the mother who embraces the family in love and care. Two paths flow from the tipi into the day. The green path represents generosity where art, dreams and domesticity are shared. The blue path represents water and sky, where ceremony, songs and animals are remembered."

Dustin Noble Red Elk Reed
Kahnawake, Mohawk Terr.
January, 2011

Our Blood Remembers

poems by

Lois Red Elk

Table of Contents

Toward Sharing a Life

by

Lois Red Elk

I have been writing since I was twelve years old (which was about fifty years ago, give or take). One of my older cousins (sixteen years old) found herself with child and very fearful of the consequences. In a note, I encouraged her to tell the truth and keep her baby. She did. That note was my first poem. My mother saved that poem and years later gave it to me. I recalled the situation where that young relative had no one to confide in except her cousin/friend. And that scene is still reenacted today. But what I saw then is that a home filled with love and care results in wanting to give back love and care, and that was all I could give my cousin at the time.

Reflecting on my childhood, I see a little girl holding Grandma's hand and walking into the "Round Hall" with smells of sage and good food in the room. After settling on several blankets over a squeaky wooden floor, we would become quieted while Grandpa called everyone to pray. I would lean up against Grandma's warm arm and listen to her words in Lakota and felt a security and happiness I thought would never end, and it hasn't. The Round Hall was an octagonal building where our community held ceremonies and meetings. It sat on the flat about a mile north of the deep woods of cottonwood and poplar thriving on the banks of Mni Sose (Missouri River). In the woods, our family had a large community garden where we collected chokecherries, bull berries, and stove wood. One of our outings into the woods is shared in the poem "When Chokecherries Turned Black."

I had five grandmothers, all sisters and half sisters. That happened because a great grandfather had three wives. I won't explain any further except to say it was an old tradition that was accepted in our culture. My own grandmother, my father's mother, passed away a year before I was born, so her four sisters became my grandmothers. I was the first born, so the grandmas made sure that I went with them to all functions — ceremonies and sewing bees (in a horse-drawn wagon), gathering berries in the woods, and at day's end I usually stayed overnight with them. The poem "Magic" is for Grandma High-Back after following her through one of her days. In putting me to bed, her description in Lakota of the day's end, the creek and the turtles, was magical and left me with a dreamlike image to ponder while going to sleep.

The grandmothers were descendants of the revered holy man Sitting Bull. Their parents were in the confrontation at "Greasy Grass" or more commonly known as "The Battle of the Little Big Horn." Being family of Sitting Bull meant the grandmothers were charged with upholding traditions by maintaining the principles Sitting Bull believed in and knew worked for the people. One of the traditions was the telling of all the old-time legends, which contained all the morals we lived by. They also knew that daily prayer could change a person, so they encourage us to pray to make us strong. The practice was also to help us learn the way of the four directions. "Grandmother Praying" is an observation of the mornings I spent with Grandma Grey Bear. Once in a while I could hear her words, and it was always for everyone and everything else except herself. I asked her about this one time, and she said in a matter of fact tone that she did this because she knew her sisters were praying for her.

My father built a log house out on Chelsea flats where my family lived. It was a community made up of about twenty families, located half way between Poplar and Wolf Point. All the families were my relatives and formed the core of upbringing for my sisters and me. Being a creative carpenter and an admitted "jack-of-all-trades," my father built us child furniture and little cradleboards for our dolls. The table we spent hours gathered around, he built. Shelves, a closet, fancy window sills—there was no end to Dad's creativity. Benches that served as chairs were also beds and storage areas. In the evenings he would sing Sioux songs. Tapping his fingers on the armchair, table, or bedstead, he would start out with a low whistling of the tune, then a hum, then sing the words of love or praise over and over. Sometimes before I pray, I repeat his ritual. It calms me and brings me to a place of reverence. He was also an excellent horseman who prided his one-man horse, a roan stallion called "Roany." He and his favorite nephew, Buddy, would both saddle up in the morning, and ride out to look for Roany. Eventually we would see Buddy coming home leading the horse without the saddle, so we knew Dad was out on the prairie somewhere with Roany, riding the hills. Later Dad would come back with stories of his adventures with rattlesnakes, coyotes and badgers, and his descriptions of rolling clouds and thunderstorms. One would think the clouds were an army of warriors. Toward late afternoon, Mom would urgently call for us girls to get into the house — Dad was coming back. I sometimes thought that the horse and Dad would be tired because Dad's approach to the house was always at a full run. We could only stand at the windows and watch as Dad jumped off his prancing horse, hanging on to the reins while the horse danced in a wide circle until the saddle strap eventually worked loose. Dad would pull the saddle off to the ground into a cloud of dust with the horse still whirling. Finally off slipped the bridle, and in a final whirl, Roany would neigh and race off toward the western sun. I remember thinking, "My Dad could ride a wild horse." The poem, "Cante-t'inswaya Manipelo" is a tribute to my father's passion and courage. He loved his horse and enjoyed observing the energy of thunderstorms.

Every other weekend, during the summer, Mom would make lemon meringue pies. For helping Dad with his horse, Buddy would get half a pie. My cousins said they could smell the aroma a mile off. The pie was made from scratch with real lemons and real egg-white meringue. Mom was also fond of crocheting. In one of my favorite pictures of my dad and me, I am wearing a crocheted dress Mom made. Her father was a real medicine man or Indian doctor. He used herbs, roots, tree bark and leaves in medicine to cure people. He also manipulated shells, bones and sacred objects in his healing practice. Mother said he also believed in a good attitude, prayer, and wholesome living — a holistic approach to healing. Mom knew his medicines and always had sweet flag, wild mint, and other herbs stored away for the appropriate time. With each medicine, she had a story. One story I always like to share is "The Deer Legend." In this book I share four poems that reflect the legacy of deer.

Mother is a Santee Sioux from the Spirit Lake Nation of North Dakota. Her early childhood was bliss. She and her cousins were allowed to roam the woods with their dogs. She was shown how to find medicine plants by her father, and she delighted in listening to her mother's songs and traditional stories in the Sioux Language. Her mother died when she was only ten years old, and soon after her father died also. Her sister who was sixteen years older and had two sons of her own, cared for her for a while, but times were very hard for everyone. Eventually she and her two little nephews were sent to parochial school. She had no choice in being placed in parochial schools and Indian boarding schools. It was barely tolerable for her. In retrospect she remembers the concise practice of forced assimilation on her people: beatings for speaking the Dakota language, removing identity by cutting off Indian braids, brainwashing to change the beliefs of Indian spirituality toward reciting scripture and catechism, public humiliation of the Indian spiritual advisors who came to visit the students, and the list goes on and on. Her young nephews both died of tuberculosis while in grade school. For twenty-five years of her early life, she tolerated ridicule by schools and the churches because of her knowledge of the Dakota language and culture. She was determined that such callous treatment was not going to change her respect for her ancestors' ways. Then, during the last half of her life, she was requested repeatedly by public schools and colleges to share that very same knowledge of Sioux culture and language. She was only too glad to share. She never lost her traditional Santee language; instead, wherever she found herself, she picked up new languages — Latin, French, some Ojibwa, Assiniboine and English. She liked to compare all the languages. She explained to me the word "Wakanyeja," which meant that as a baby I was born pure, not sinful. That poem "Wakanyeja" is in her memory. I and my husband were living in Los Angeles when I had my first child. It was after this that she and her sister decided to have a song made for me by one of her cousins from Spirit Lake. In receiving the song, I was also given instructions to aid me in my walk in L.A. The poem "Toward Traveling" is part of those guiding instructions. In her last days, it was the Indian Medicine men who came to her in visions. In sharing this with me, she was rightfully glad.

My tribal nation is considered the fourth largest in the country, next to the Navajo, the Cherokee, and Choctaw. We are known as a warrior people, and that we are. So much is written about my people, sometimes in the past tense with the message that our way of life was annihilated after the Indian wars, or that we are the idols of the new age "wannabe" sweat lodgers. They either want us dead or want to copy our ways. When I am a guest speaker, I tell people that the Indian Nations are growing, culture is alive and maintaining, and we do not condone people who take parts of our culture and exploit it for profit. For example, the man who allowed several people to die in a sweat lodge ritual that was of his own making. Some "Movie Makers" and self appointed gurus belong in the same category — exploiters of culture. The poems "One of These Days," and "For Thieves Only" are in rebuttal to the exploiters.

Unfortunately, so many of my people have been denied the right to know their culture and then generations later they have become the statistics of many social ills. There is no denying that the government and churches have done their share of harm. I wrote "A Force They Could Not Control" after hearing the testimony from a survivor of the boarding schools. "Not All Ghosts Are Dead" came to me after listening to some of my Catholic relatives, and "Images of What you Hate" is about a dear friend's sorrowful but now recovering life from alcoholism.

In deciding what to title my book, I was given the answer as I was resting one day. I had to attend a late meeting and decided to take a quick nap. Just as I was awakening, I heard Sitting Bull say, "Remember our blood." I analyzed that to mean that I was to be a representative of our people and share the good ways of our Nation. The poem, "Our Blood Remembers" is my doctrine that blood and genes have memory and these memories speak to us all the time, if we will listen.

At the end of this book I've included some of my favorite D/Lakota words from the Sioux

Nation. Growing up I heard the dialects of the Mdewakanton, Wahpekute, Pabaksa, Hunkpapa and Ihanktowan (Yankton) in the home. These dialects are branches of what is called the Seven Council fires or bands that make up the great Sioux Nation. The Isanyati (Santee) say they are the original band of Sioux and lived in the east along the coast. My mother heard languages from some of those tribes and could understand because of the root words and word endings. It is all very interesting and awesome to me. Recently the Oglala Lakota published an all inclusive dictionary of the Sioux language. It is called *New Lakota Dictionary* and incorporates the Dakota dialects of the Yankton-Yanktonai and Santee Sisseton. I enjoy reading it, but only a page at a time. It is a 20,000 word volume book, and includes over 40,000 example sentences.

My Mother passed to the spirit world about eight years ago. My father died at age forty-eight of a massive heart attack. Though they are gone, their spirits are always with me. Sometimes in dreams they relay messages to me, and they come near in times of need. They are also present when I am absolutely enjoying myself. I know they join me in my joy. Because of their sacred beliefs and love of the Dakota and Lakota they would want me to share the beauty of our culture.

Mom loved to read and admired teachers, and her wish was that I would become a teacher. Before she passed, I graduated from Rocky Mountain College with a Bachelor Degree in Education. That new knowledge assisted me in developing curriculum based on Sioux culture. Today I'm an Adjunct Professor and teach courses on traditional Native American medicines, animals significant to the culture, the art of porcupine quillwork, and other Native American topics.

The fourth section of the book is called Iwahoiciya — We Promise. "We" the ancestors, relatives, family and I were all committed at birth to live in harmony with the plants, animals and all that God has created. And after harmony, the promise continues toward healing, recovering, unifying, sharing, and respecting. My parents and grandmas would want me to share with all of you that the spirits or angels, which are attached to God, still see us humans walking holy, because we were made in the greatest sacred ceremony of all. Those all-knowing, all-seeing sacred grandmothers and grandfathers, those representatives of God, are always with us and will see us through to the next world. The poem "They Still See Us" speaks about how we are never alone. And it is our right to move toward sharing that good knowledge while on this earthly walk.

Lois Red Elk (Reed)
Moon of Popping Trees
Late January and early February, 2011

This book is dedicated to my father's mother, "Brings Her Sorrel Horse," and her four sisters — the one's who taught me the traditional Lakota lifeways — Grandmothers "Highback," "Grey Bear," "Two Bonnet," and "Silver." Also to my father, "Back Tracks His Horses," and my mother, "Sacred Voice Woman," who cherished their first born.

— Lois Red Elk

I have been waiting a long time — perhaps even my whole lifetime — for this collection of poems. It is as if we have all been given the gift of time and perspective, allowed to view our world, our lives, our strengths and shortcomings through a primeval and potent lens. If we are to endure, persist and thrive again, we need these words. As lucid as a spring thunderstorm on the high plains, Red Elk's candor, clarity and wisdom are imparted amongst and across generations. This collection is what we have all been waiting for.

— Mandy Smoker Broaddus

It is important that you write in your own Indigenous language when you compose your poetry; that is the genuine voice of our people. It is so important that our own people appreciate and use their own language; that, to me, is where the real poetry of Indigenous spirit, mind, heart, soul is. Our Indigenous language is the true voice of our land, culture, and community, and it is the voice of poetry truly.

— Simon J. Ortiz

I. Dakod Wicohan (Dakota Culture)

Blanket of Song and Culture

With united minds and spirits of many generations,
the society aided by turtles and lizards, praying with
a sweetgrass braid, welcomed the first born of the
man with many horses and the woman of spring
flowers. Joined by scarlet plumes and sacred smoke
the couple received the four spirits that entered earth's
plain like a fast moving fire ball. Sent by the maker
of ancestor stars, a new life took residence among
all her relations. Wrapped in the red blanket of song,
and culture, mother and father lifted their voices
and took the vow of the pierced ears ritual to teach
and raise their child in the good Lakota way.

Wakanyeja	**Sacred Gift (a child)**
Apetu ki	This day
wicin cana wan ici mani	a female traveler has arrived
kimiminawa	a butterfly
omaki yaka	said to me
Apetu ki	This day
wana hi	she has arrived
Mitakana	My little sister
wanyaka	behold
Apetu ki	This day
wicin cana wan ici mani	a female traveler has arrived
Wakanyeja	A sacred gift
wana hi	has arrived
Mitakuyapi	My relatives
wanyaka	behold
Wakanyeja	A sacred gift
wana hi	has arrived

Note: A female traveler has arrived means a baby girl has been born. This poem was written on the arrival of my youngest granddaughter.

Magic

She sent dusk down Tule Creek with the
turtles then arranged by feather tick bed.

"Time to let go of the day," she whispered
as she lowered the glowing kerosene lamp.

The old woods standing guard behind her house
reflected branches and wind in her dark eyes.

Holding me in silence close to her pillowed body
she was solid and warm as the afternoon ground.

Her heart, a steady "round dance" beat
soothed my mind from clouds to magic.

Speaking Sioux to approaching storms today
she scolded thunder, offered meat to lightning.

I asked why? She said, "Dream about it."
I nodded, sighed and thought about rain.

I followed one gray hair to the edge of her smile,
As her patient breathing rocked my body quiet.

Grandmother Praying

Every morning it was a ritual; I would hear her stirring,
knew she was putting on her moccasins, bed creaking
told me she was collecting her hair into one long braid,
nimble fingers flexing then pulling a robe around her

motherly frame. Her breathing was steady but hurried,
sometimes a cough or a hum, to let us know she was
beginning her time with the new day. The door would
open quietly, fresh air would flush through the rooms,

then out the back windows leaving sweet smells of
dew on morning grass. These moments that have been
imprinted in my mind, I bring back weekly, make
them my own present knowledge, my faith. I see

where she is standing alongside our old log house,
watch the morning breeze lift loose hairs around her
temples into fine ripples. Her dark eyes receive spirits
who dwell in sun's rays, just above earth and warmly

mingle with quivering poplar leaves and songs of
meadowlark and robin. To the east, where all life
begins, she raises a hand to touch the Great Spirit's
space, the place where connection is made with the

sacred world. In her other hand she carries a small
braided circle of sweet grass—Mother Earth's generously
imparted, fragrant hair—her communion offering from
the mortal to ancestors and angels. Grandmother's

whisper softly unifies with the essence of increasing
light, her greeting, her acknowledgment of the sacredness
has begun. Two slight steps and her body faces south.
She bows in reverence, humbly lowering her face as a

common human being portraying the difficulty to stand
upright before the moving power of the creator. A tear
slides to the soil, another sacrifice from her frail stature
as she asks forgiveness for the failures of her people and

her offspring. She knows the difficulty of maintaining
custom and practice, how insistent dark energies pry away
loved ones from wisdom and grace to error and ignorance.
And she knows this direction of growth will win the battle,

that all will be forgiven and restored. Her body
straightens and is strengthened as she meets the west,
meets that dark strength approaching and forming
into healing clouds. It is where the infinite voice of

Thunderbird's lightning oath will bring renewal.
Grandmother knows that source of replenishing rain
brings needed purification. She thanks all the powers
who will quench the thirst of all life. And she knows

she too will have the comfort of thunder's blessing. She
has come full circle. The peace of the north welcomes
her and her prayers — that tireless course she claims as
wont. She will witness and celebrate abundant rewards

for a people reclaiming birthright, then receiving the fruit
of supplication. That sacred journey through the morning,
the universe has been with the Great Spirit as direction,
her devotion in life. She knows this has always been the

true spirit of her people. This day, that collective spirit,
that humble utterance from a woman dedicated to her
ancestry, is brought before eternity, before the witness
of the all knowing, loving entity, beholding for all time.

When Chokecherries Turned Black

It was a magical time, yes a time of survival, but we knew
it as fun, being together, being with the grandmas, a time
to learn some good lessons and beautiful songs in the old
tongue — Lakota Sioux. All my young female relatives and
I busied ourselves putting together bags to carry our

chokecherries. Mother cut a pillowcase in half, stitched
up the ends and added drawstrings. We pretended we
were adults, fussed over each other, showed how to carry
the bags, how to sit and pick the best — proud of our skills.
Our Grandma High-Back had a bag made of deer skin and

another grandma had one made of fawn skin. We admired
how they wore them, a padded strap around their neck,
and shoulder, efficient for plucking, for all the ripe beauty
handled with care. We started for the woods just after the
sun came over the trees. Grandma had two big dogs who

were always along. They had small 'travois' strapped to
their backs, were always anxious to go somewhere, to be
part of the "Chokecherry Party," so obedient, patient, never
chased the rabbits or mice. The Grandmas walked ahead
on the trail through the willows and brush, parted the tall

grasses, kept us close, reminded us of ticks, ants, or thorns,
of all the little dangers in our world of adventure. One
auntie followed behind, carrying a branch of poplar leaves,
swatting away the flies, mosquitoes, and other biting things.
Walking to the chokecherry patch was like walking into a

new world. The berry bushes were taller every year, so
plentiful, unrecognizable. Once there the adults would
start singing, one after the other. It was like a joyous
greeting, an exchange, a beginning into a beautiful
time and space of fragrant leaves and abundant branches.

The Grandmas had mellow voices, a gentle breeze weaving in and out of what seemed like hundreds of songs. I don't remember any sounding the same, a new song telling a new story for a new year. All of we little ones, anxious, would sit on the ground and pick the bottom cherries while

the Grandmas picked the cherries closer to the sky. As I looked up they looked plump and glossy like little gopher eyes. Soon our cheeks bulged with sweet, juicy fruit. We would fill our bags then pour them into larger bags attached to the travois. When we began to slow down and

tire we would all stop and have a bite to eat. The bags turned into a full spread of food and wild mint tea. The Grandmas all spoke in Sioux and would tell funny stories about each other. Sometimes we didn't understand the entire joke, but their untamed laughter made us giggle.

We laughed so hard we had to stand and hold our sides. After we had picked for another hour or so, we would head home — Grandmas in front, the dogs pulling the loaded travois and us kids. Sometimes my younger sister would fall asleep so she got to ride with all the

sweet smelling bags. About five households shared the cherries. Each grandma had her own special set of pounding stones, like a mortar and pestle. It seemed like the grandmas worked on cherries for a week, pounding, grinding and shaping the cherry pulp into patties, then

setting them out to dry in the baking July sun until they became hard and black. Eventually all the dried patties were placed in large pieces of cheese cloth, tied-up into bundles and stored hanging from the rafters. All winter long we enjoyed eating chokecherry pudding, sometimes

chokecherries mixed with dried deer meat, or a sauce over deer roast, chokecherry soup with dried cracklings of pork, and chokecherry jam and jelly. My grandmas liked to cook. They cooked to honor the seasonal moon, the moon when the chokecherries turned black.

The Deer Legend

"Tell us about Deer Woman, Dad. Tell us about the power she possessed. Does she really come at night to whisper secrets to the uncles and brothers? How do you hunt them?"

"Deer have excellent hearing and have ears that constantly twitch back and forth. They are able to sense danger right away. I hunt them on foot when alone. I tie my horse to a tree branch, stand perfectly still, scan the brush, then walk into the woods. I also have excellent hearing and eyesight. I can identify what animals are around and I can smell the sweet odor of deer. I know where the deer trails are, the seasons not to take them and am so quick I can rope them sometimes. I was taught at an early age. I remembered. But deer are tricky too and circle around and even attack. They can do a lot of damage if they get behind you."

"But Grandma said deer are magical. She said they take care of you. They kill snakes. How do they do that?"

"Deer have large beautiful eyes that look pure and good. If they can get you to stare into their eyes, you feel sorry for them and spare their lives. One-time I witnessed a doe kill a large rattler that was crawling near her fawn. The doe pounced over and over on the snake with her hooves until it quit moving. She was protecting her young one."

"I want to see them. Can sister and me visit with them?"

"One day a deer will visit you in your dreams. She will bring you good knowledge about the porcupine and how to use its quills to embroidery or she'll teach you how to do fine beadwork or how to make beautiful moccasins. When this happens you have to pay attention and do what your dream tells you. You'll have to tell your grandma."

“Tell us more stories. Tells us about the time Deer Woman visited uncle, scared him so he couldn’t sleep.”

“One night he heard women talking outside his window. The next day when he went outside to look where they were talking, all he saw were deer tracks. Sometimes women can be heard giggling in the brush while we are out hunting, but there are usually only deer hoof prints found in the soft dirt. She wasn’t playing tricks on your uncle she was trying to bring him the power to call horses, but he wasn’t ready to hear good things. He just wanted to see if she was beautiful. If he could take her out.”

“I want to dream about the deer. I’m going to bed early.”

Dakota Deer Language

This Man learned the language of deer, felt the tongue of a four-legged possess his mouth and thinking, came at a time when his mind was wide open like the smoke flaps of his tipi. The heat and the pleasure of his scent drifted out and over the land signaling the sensitive and alert.

Walking a distance from camp one day, clouds began pulling in a storm. Tired and hurrying, he approached a clearing in the woods. In the arms of distant trees he recognized his camp. Suddenly the woods amassing black revealed a strange woman. She appeared like the one in his dreams, the one he desired, offered gifts to the spirits for. The beauty stood draped, a buffalo robe over one shoulder. Her silky, black hair touched the ground. He felt hoof beats under his chest. Thought his mind dreamed him quickly to another place. He approached the friendly woman; they spoke and passed the time like they knew each other. He playfully wrapped his rope around her pretending she would stay, or want to live with him forever.

Suddenly, there was a stirring in the woods. Back from gathering berries, children and pets emerged, a dog barked and frightened the would-be woman. All beauty was startled and struggled against the rope. She tried to leap, hurl herself toward the woods. Suddenly her robe parted and revealed the shadow of a deer, ears twitching. Not a woman's shadow, not flowing hair, not a rounded body among buckskin fringes. Instead it was the shadow of the alert, hair covered, listening and wanting to move quickly on four legs.

The man, confused, threatened to kill her. She pleaded for her being, cried strange sparkling tears, promised anything for her spirit, her offspring, her legend, she promised to give the man powers beyond belief.
When the man let go of the beauty, he let go of emotion. Letting go of his fear, he created his future. Running toward the woods, feeling the push of four legs renewed her life. Now all she wanted was to put distance between her spirit and the disbelief of the human

He returned to camp, not knowing how or where he had been, but strangely sure he had seen another world. He questioned what he gained from a place he thought he dreamed, thought he felt and embraced. Why did his body only vomit and his mind lose time? Times he would feel better, and then disorder would start all over again. Why did he have this urge to whistle, run away? leap, and feel the bushes on his legs? And, why did the woods smell so fresh, so appealing. How strange his purge, his deer cycle.

The people were sad. He used to be a fine man, did hunting for the people, fed the elders and needy. That's how he fed his needs. And, he always looked for a woman to love and care for, one who would give him children, gifts and love.

Finally the people created a lodge for him, like the wisdom of the womb, made of heat, mist, purity and growth. Exploding rocks and medicine herbs were placed before his face. The ancestors spoke to him from the voice of eternity, and it was in rebirth that he came back to his human mind.

He lived alone, haunted and dreaming of the uncommon woman, how she once stood before him, long hair, dark oval eyes, and soft skin. Times when the vision became so unbearable he would lift his voice and his singing would bring him horses, beautiful horses of all colors. Their neighing was like the uncoiling wind. They pranced to a hum radiating from earth's center. Their manes, shiny like human hair, flowed and twisted into ropes down their backs, stirring up the soil and stirring the passion of knowledge.

Through the songs he heard the woman's voice sending a song of gratitude, a woman's promise. In exchange for her freedom she gave him the power to beckon horses. Now his eyes are allowed to believe the miracle of custom, his tongue speaks a rare truth, now the legend is his. And, for all those who hunger for belief, for something to hang on to, still few will listen to the language of truth, of culture — the endowment of deer woman.

Calling Horses Song

My sister, come outside, listen to my song.
Come listen to my song.

On this new day I am calling some horses.
Come, I am calling some horses.

Dawn is rising; the west wind is blowing.
Come, the west wind is blowing.

My Sister, see the many horses coming.
Come see the many horses coming.

Sunka Wakan Wacipedo (The Horses are Dancing)

Otokaya kagapi,
Otokaya kagapi,
Otokaya kagapi,
Tehan amautan.

The creation,
The creation,
The creation,
You looked at us.

Sunka Wakan ahodawo,
Sunka Wakan ahodawo,
Sunka Wakan ahodawo,
Mini wicakuwo.

Respect the horses,
Respect the horses,
Respect the horses,
Give them water.

Sunka Wakan kuwanto,
Sunka Wakan kuwanto,
Sunka Wakan kuwanto,
Wanyaka duzah han.

Horses, come over here,
Horses, come over here,
Horses, come over here.
See their swift running.

Sunka Wakan wacipedo,
Sunka Wakan wacipedo,
Sunka Wakan wacipedo
Eced waste wacipedo.

The horses are dancing,
The horses are dancing,
The horses are dancing,
And they're dancing well.

At Winter Solstice

We
have all
risen at this moment,
sometimes in a dream or in a
distant thought to meet the hour when
light and dark retrieve time from the icy north.
We have found ourselves beholding the absence of
that disc of fire, of life and we have yearned for a common
warmth, a light to assure our quiet direction. It is
when time turns into a whisper, when we exhale
descending crystals of night and breathe
into our lives the early rays of the
new day that we know we
have walked the earth in
the sacred span of
solstice.

Winter Count

Now the days are dim, flakes drift down in
place of light. A chill passes over my
shoulders, sends me to find the knowledge of
foxes asleep in quiet places where dried
sweet grass and sage lie hidden in dreams,
keeping spirit alive throughout the long night.

My solitude is seen as a single stream of
breath in morning air, the sole sign of my
existence. Only the morning star has mercy,
understands this need to reflect from a space
so distant. Tonight I'll drape my body with
star quilts in honor of our endurance.

I watch that old fire journey lower across
earth; listen to their whispers — secrets of
retreat and renewal, their celestial bond.
I assign myself to a pace of spirit and mind
that surpasses the counted risings and settings,
then put envy to sleep with my longing for flame.

As the ancient one settles, dress of swirling
fog, breath of crystallized vapor and spreads his
northern robe, my heart makes peace with resting,
I'll recall the night of foxes and stars, my eager
reach for warmth, then watch for new grass rising
through melting snow. This is my winter count.

II. Woiyotiyekiye (A Difficult Time)

Hit by Hard Times

It was as if a people were set up with a bulls's-eye branded on their chest and back. No matter if they walked or ran, no matter if they were abiding or working, they were hit. Hit by another man's quest for freedom, hit by a poison the pure genes could not tolerate, hit by disease and death, hit by isolation and disappearances. Then they were told they had to play the bureau game — declare yourself unworthy, incompetent and they would take care of you. It was just a matter of time before love was replaced with hitting and abuse, before the Indian culture was traded for an alcoholic culture. The abused became the abuser. This is called hard times.

Not All Ghosts Are Dead

Some still move secretly among Indian homes, waiting for the proper time to release rage. A kind of rage that builds and overcomes, taking over all human senses. One minute it is calm, the women remembering the childhood of playing, laughing, of merry voices, but growing too loud, the present turning shades of darkness. Dark pages begin to call up distant circles in the women's eyes, spinning from past to present until hearts beat out of control. They begin reliving all the beatings over and over. Finally, that secret little scream, bloodied and stifled since those terrible childhood times, slips out again for what they had hoped was the last time. This present laughter that is so unbearable has to stop like the time nuns whirled into the room with hairbrushes, rulers and straps, beating little brown skin, little fingers and little exposed cheeks, exposure hurting as bad as the repeated lifting of holy white hands coming down constantly, down on little Indian girls for singing, sharing, speaking and being all they ever knew. But, the rage doesn't stop there, it merges when it is least expected. Now the adult children of the children have identified and can control the cruel rush after the laughter, but they never knew when fear took the place of what was lost — how to cry, how to trust, how to pray — never knew why they took up the beating, when they became the inheritors of the strange catechism. The women are too old now to be beaten, but they wonder when the haunting will stop. They wait somewhere below God, below ancient burial scaffolds, below crosses, asking the ghosts of nuns to release the souls of the pitiful little school girls, those who have suffered the torture long enough.

A Force They Could Not Control

The buildings are gone now.
Not a planned demolition, but
a matter of structures slowly
wasting away. Now, only the
brown and gray pictures remain,
left in boxes in the attics of
abandoned buildings and
in the minds of young children
now in bodies fully grown.

Set up by the war department,
a school for the children
of the beguiled and helpless,
taught to sew, to mend shoes,
to be carpenters or farmers,
and to touch secretly,
so that no one would know.
It was after all a school; and
they learned their lessons well.

The witnesses: places
quiet and cold; the kitchen, the pantry,
the dark, dank basement.
Tear-stained faces, one by one.
One who closed his eyes real tight;
One whose face would turn blue;
One who lost his speech;
One fearful of running water.

The descendants sort through
old photographs; each face a memory.
This one became a rancher,
-rode the hell out of his horses.
This one killed himself,
-before his eighteenth birthday.
This one drank until he passed out.
And that one, that one,
passed on the legacy of touch.

They were told not to tell, but
they have, and look for their
lives in pictures and see
the cunning that taught them
touch and how to win the
trust of children. And they did not
know that the touch would
lead them to the time when they too
would look upon the children with

a force they could not control.

Have You Been There?

It was an inevitable move,
had to know why he stayed.
Answer came from the ones
who said they'd been there.
They pointed to the back of
the room. There, halls, dim,
turned left and right. At the
end was a stairway, steep,
led deeper and darker.
Eyes, wide, couldn't focus
through layers of blue haze.
Voices were recognized as
slurred, human and I saw
shapes, sitting, hunched,
in the same manner, on
equal stools. No movement,
no vision, no color, just
stools, stinking stools,
stools with holes filled to
the brim. Someone hollered
out, "Hey, what are you
doing in a place like this?"
I'm told to sit, try to sit,
need to, but the crap keeps
floating higher, shoes getting
soaked. A grinning face
questioned, "How do you
like it here? You think you
know why he's here? How
do you know? You don't
know shit!" And, that's
all they said. They all
laughed, denied there was
a problem and kept on
sipping. They did, however,
defend their right to say,
"We've been there. We know
what it's all about."

Images of What You Hate

I listen to a voice pulled
tight and watch a red mist
float from your raw throat,
words chilled by too much
drink yet trying to think.
I want to reach you, but
find you swallowing my
life, piece by piece, into
that lonely place, a gut
full of cigarette butts,
bloated and losing color,
and discover the one who
wished she never birthed
you still haunting your dry
times, tipping a bottle over
that gaping hole in the middle
of your soul time after
time with promises smelling
like cheap wine, and kisses
tasting like stale wishes.
The only sure thing was
hearing the clank of six
packs, till your voice took
up the same ring, bringing
dread to the ones you named
chips off the ol' keg. Their
believing turning into dead
weight, too numb to relate.
Their eyes, half tears, half
stone are looking at images,
images of what you said
you'd never become — images
of what you hate.

He Said He Knows

Outlasting all his buddies, he
knows every alley, and
every shortcut
between hunger
and a place
to sleep.
Shiny streets from evening
rain reflect a dark form
standing between
sidewalk and
survival.
He asks for a quarter, and
you know it isn't going
to buy his way back
to Kyle.
It was his eyes that stopped
me, scanning my face like
liquor absorbed relatives —
embarrassed, but
pleading,
that reflection of hope that
died and came back over
and over, leaving soul
just this side of the
cemetery.
His blood could come from chiefs
or a mother's prayer, but right
now, with wine and beer
long evaporated from
veins and brow, the
chief needs to
replenish his
blood by
tilting
a jug.

I reach for a dollar, pull
up a five, give it anyway
and turn away — won't
question or accept
where he's
been.
He reaches for my hands,
I'm not frightened off,
feel a tired Indian
spirit cradle my
fingers.
He said he knows who
he is, and when he
dies he will ride
alongside
Crazy
Horse.

Caged Separately

Caged separately, they pace close to the wire,
sometimes in the opposite direction, but always
they meet at the same hole in the fence hoping
they'll find a way through the next time around.

With anxious eyes, they look like they just came
back from near death but want to attend another life,
another approach, beyond this point. When his
would-be mate shuts her eyes, he dips and pushes

his chest over the ground, scents twigs and grass
with invitations. She observes his movement
through the leaves and begins to dig. She digs
hard and deep, breaks nails, limbs cake with dirt

trying to figure a way to get at him. To no avail,
she gives up. This is his season, his habit. She
knows the set up. She waits for the time when
small, furry, unsuspecting ones enter their domain.

The wolves become challenged to a game they
know well. Both skilled at the hunt (calling it
survival and getting even) they inspect how each
charm and pace, how each will satisfy need. At

times the victim becomes a plaything and is tossed
at the wire. They watch, then plan the final kill.
Starting with warm saliva dripping, aroused tails
quivering thighs, the two take up the game. No one

stands a chance. All are targets. When it's all over;
she tries in vain to lick his wounds. She lunges
desperately at the fence, in a kind of passion, only
to be bounced back by blood messages to the body

and senses. She's tried and tried, it doesn't work.
The fence wears dark offerings of ripped flesh and
fur, a sign of how much they care. During the
season of the moon, they pant and howl in unison

(loving and hating the one they love and hate).
Two of a kind, they rub brow and back on wire
knots, pretending blue metal is tongue to soothe
canine tension, then retreat one more time to lean

against each other, the ever present barrier
between their lives, and lower faces to cages.

Tonight the Fists

Tonight the fists will start.
Those warm loving fingers
will roll inward, tight and
terrible. Tonight the beater
will use all the energy saved
from hating yesterday's night,
leftover from remembering
when father's fists first arose,
the pounding echoing from
ear to ear, when lips turned
red, the red spread, when
beautiful Indian cheekbones
turned blue and bulged. His
eyes, wide and wild became
her mirrors, where she saw a
fleeing female form, cowering,
pleading, saw how the head
became a symbol for women,
all women for those he loved,
feared with his mouth, his
heart, his legs, his wounds.
Saw when no one believed
that the white collar, the quiet,
average man, took his place
among the gentle. But your
tears knew the trembling quiet,
the pending storm, the last
straw, when you bargained
with time, you lost every time,
and you spoke with angels.

Don’t Pass My Sister Love Around

Don’t pass
my sister
love around,
like some
goddamned
joint,
inhaled for
a selfish
high, then
blown like a
whim into
oblivion.
My fiber
sizzles to
the core, it
crackles and
burns. You
burn me up!
You’ve got
my precious
time deep
in your lungs
and you’re
hanging on
for some
desperate
knowledge.
My patience
is as fragile
as rolling
paper.
I won’t be
around for
the next toke.

The Lives of Deer Woman

It was the approach of something dying that hurried me
home. I saw her, in the distant or immediate future, a

wounded deer thrashing in the brush. She had wandered
into the city, lured by the dream of a human, the kind who

say they honor the earth, make it safe for her to live. But
the welcoming dreamer wasn't that kind, clouded his mind

from time to time, tried to treat her like fair game. On his
way to fooling her, he fell under her spell. She thought he

understood her deer spirit, wanted to walk his path awhile,
almost lost her tradition when she took a drink of his dark

water. The drink sent her mind into a field of hunters,
sharp teeth snapped at her legs, peeled her skin, threw her

head in the trash. Terrified, she woke up, wanted to go
home, looked for her pouch of twigs and grass, found her

dreamer holding on to her spirit like she was a savior. He
thought she was a wish come true, to love all his illusions,

to soothe each time he used his pain. She tried to speak
her language, knowing how to rid life of lies and snakes,

how to call upon purifying rain. He called her style myth,
only felt safe among his own, needed a bottle to calm his

confusion. Waking in the middle of the night he saw her
deer shadow, lost his grasp and fired into his dream come

true. Headshot would have eased this journey, but
she wasn't a human spirit and she knows human spirits

can linger, can wander on and on. Instead, a lung was
bruised and a limb shattered, ripping and breaking was

delayed by muscle. I watched her try to get up, be brave,
like nothing happened, or pretend her leg could carry her

away. She saw a need for order, to slow her heart, maybe
in the shelter of trees. But she was getting weaker,

kept falling, each fall a setback, breaking ribs, each rib
hurting unprotected skin, killing her slowly. Her eyes,

once pure, now bewildered; breath, once sweet, labored,
as blood words forced into her throat and leaked from

her nose begging to the sixth sense for a kind of resolve.
The last time I saw her, she was escaping through the lobby,

onto the street, and back to her world to tell of survival —
the lives of deer woman, who chanced to trust in those

who could believe. The dreamer? Denies he sees her,
says it's restless sleep. Yet when he hears her deer

whistle he thinks she's back, that dream that got away.

One of These Days

One of these days,
I'm going to that kitchen drawer
full of scalping knives,
pick a few sharp ones and
slip 'em into my sock.

Then I'm heading for the hall closet,
where all my tomahawks are hanging,
select a couple of heavy ones, and
shove 'em under my belt.

I'm gonna arm myself to my gleaming teeth!

Then I'm going to the freezer,
pull out a variety of scalps —
maybe seven or eight — and
hang 'em around my neck.

And what about all that war paint?
Some purple lipstick will do just fine.
And those yellow and green turkey feathers?
glue 'em to my head.

Oh yes, the blood curdling scream.
I've got that too! (being sick and tired)
And about the flaming arrows? Just like me,
they burned up.

Now all I need is a
60-inch television screen.
One of these days, I'm gonna do my thing,
maybe after the next commercial.

For Thieves Only

Don't tell me your great, great
grandmother is an Indian Princess!

This Indian's cheekbones have
been kicked by hate.
This hawk shaped nose has
smelled her parent's fear.
This redskin's hands smothered
a baby to protect a nation.

I paid the price.
I know terror.
I took a life.

Don't tell me your great, great
grandmother is an Indian Princess!

This raven hair has been caked with blood,
and the color was never lost.
This heathen soul was nailed by a cross,
and the earth is still my relative.
This Indian heart was betrayed for 500 years,
and my people have continued.

I refuse dishonor.
I am tradition.
I have survived.

I am as keen as a diamond back —
know the coming of thieves.
Meet me at my children's feet,
I'll show you what you never learned.

Grass Dancing

Grass, dancing north of Route 66, whispers
secrets of survival on a low west wind.
Only you and I hear them, see them — the
apparitions holding our attention, reminding
us of when we first honored the grasses
flourishing and in abundance. Our winter
was hard. The ones "Pure from the Great
Spirit," died — mother's breasts were dry.
The "Long Living," lungs fragile, no buffalo
broth to carry spirit, passed on. Finally, old
hides and old moccasins were boiled for
the youth and men. Then we ate our dogs.
They knew their sacrifice, that they would
become legend to remind the greedy and
keep us humble. It was the first sighting of
new grasses that made us cry. Tears came,
washing away the horrible night, because
some had died, because we had persisted.
We picked bunches of grass, tied them to
our back and belt, to our arms, legs, and
danced for joy and love that grandmother
earth turned for our life. "When grasses
are plenty, there will be plenty all around,"
is the secret whispered on that spring wind.

III. Ukiya (Returning)

To Come Back

If one chooses to look very carefully, after the
intense inferno, after the smoke clears, there
among the embers and ash, one can watch the
arrival of a single blade of grass. One can see
the careful pace of beetle legs revisiting new
life. Then one can hear the lone restored song
of the meadowlark, and inhale the fresh smell of
the homecoming rain. It is then, in the assembling
and mending that it will be safe to come back
to who you were meant to be. In that time.

Our Blood Remembers

The day the earth wept, a quiet wind covered the
lands weeping softly like an elderly woman, shawl
over bowed head. We all heard, remember? We were
all there. Our ancestral blood remembers the day
Sitting Bull, the chief of chiefs, was murdered. His
white horse quivered as grief shot up through the
crust of hard packed snow. Guardian relatives mourned
on our behalf. They knew our loss, took the pain from
our dreams, left us with our blood. We were asked to
remember the sweeter days, when leaves and animals
reached to touch him as he passed by. You know those
times, to reach for a truth only the pure of heart
reflect. Remember the holy man — peace loving. He
was a sun dancer — prayed for the people, water, land and
animals. Blessed among the blessed, chosen to lead the
people, he showed us the good red road, the one that
passes to our veins from earth through pipestone. Our
blood remembers. In vision he foresaw the demise of
that man, the one with yellow hair. "Soldiers falling
upside down into camp," he saw. Champion of the people,
a visionary, he taught us how to dream, this ancestor
of our blood. He instructed, "Let us put our minds
together to see what life we will make for our children" —
those pure from God. Remember? Pure from God, the
absolute gift, from our blood and blessed by heaven's
stars. And, we too, pure from God, our spirit, our blood,
our minds and our tongues. The sun dancer knew this,
showed us how to speak the words and walk the paths
our children would follow. Remember?

Grandmother, Remind Us

Lay us down upon your heart one more time so we may remember where we come from. Grandmother Earth, show us the way back to the beginning, to creation's gate when we were Spirits in one with Woniyawakan, let us relearn the instructions of the quilled Cekpapi — the dedication and promise of the turtle and lizard to our youth. We know you cradled us in your womb. We too were born of clay, of spirit, of WakanTanka. We too were sacred gifts in the genesis. We are now willing to return to the sacred waters to receive instruction from the night of salamanders. Show us the liquid blue streams of our mother. Let us witness how the blue turned red as our blood spread into the likeness of the amazing creator. Raise your voice to the pitch of shattering crystal so we may never forget the songs of the birthing chant. Thank the Tunkansina for sending the winds from the four directions, for breathing into our bodies so we may have movement on your sacred back. Tell us the stories of salamander's relatives, how Turtle extends your loving care to the infant girls, how Lizard brings your code of wisdom and healthy living to the infant boys. We know the cosmos contributed to the infant souls and only Creator allows the little ones to travel to this place, to live in our care. Remind us of their travel, that they are pure beings, to be loved and raised with ceremony, to be nourished with the old knowledge, and taught to honor the gods above and below and to honor the first mother, our grandmother earth. Lead us back to the river, back to the edge of Mother's water where salamanders, turtles and lizards wait to remind us of our duties, our vow, to care for creator's gifts — the children.

Notes:

Woniyawakan — Holy Spirit.
Cekpapi — Umbilical cord.
WakanTanka — God.
Tunkansina — Grandfathers.

Toward Traveling

The ceremony was complete. Unci
placed sage on her hair as she drifted
toward dreaming. A wave of warmth
surrounded her face becoming the unified
breath of Lakota women spirits singing
praises on the wind. Custom will now
become earth-living in a unified direction.
It was during the moon when trees
shake off their leaves when language
on steady brown tongues beckoned
movement toward the earth center
of all that is. Time was about ghosts
pointing to roads red, black, yellow and
white. Her course explained she climbed
the back of thunder's four-legged. Her
green shawl fringes, like whips, caressed
the back draft of her fast moving horse,
licked her legs, encouraged flanks as she
drifted toward the foreheads of ancient
buffalo turning into hills covered in dark
growth, hint of pine replacing air and wind.
It was there among the new blood of the
one called Inkpaduta and the true followers
of Tatanka Iyotaka that the woman who
Waters Her Horses dutifully spread her
shawl of generosity and humbly gave
her life to the knowing path of star people.
Upon arrival the Ikceya Wicasa and all
those who breathe and exhale life spirit
welcomed the young woman to the realm
of Grandmother Earth's eternal motion.

Notes:

Unci — Grandmother, the blood, earth and body of the Sioux.
Inkpaduta — Scarlet Point, Mdewakantonwan Chief.
Tatanka Iyotaka — Sitting Bull, Hunkpapa Medicine Man.
Ikceya Wicasa — Common Man, what the Dakota/Lakota call themselves.

Red Fire Ants

Among the hills and pines, teen problems swarm the land
like red fire ants on their way to nowhere or somewhere,

a motion known only to them, but determined and relentless.
We know where they came from, rode in on whiskey crates

and pack mules. For years they grew in numbers. No one
tried to stop them because they were red. Then they begin

to bite and devour everything in sight. Red fire ants gambled
the food money. Red fire ants snorted the diaper money.

Red fire ants drank up the tennis shoe money. Red fire ants
toked up the utility bill money. Teen problems? Yes! They

get up to feed the kids, go to work to diaper the kids, hustle
to buy shoes for the kids, steal and sell to get spending money

for the kids. Teens try to take root in something, stand their
ground, some do, but some can be eaten alive or carried

away in pieces. So, for today, hang on to the passing horses,
they will teach you about companionship and commitment.

Hang on to the low flying eagles, they will teach you about
prayer and spiritual places. Hang on to the grazing black tail

deer, they will teach you family responsibility. Hang on to
stomping buffalo, they will teach you to live the beautiful

way. Hang on to the diving red tail hawk, it will teach you
to handle your problems immediately. The animals know

this valley the best. They see what's going on and they,
they will lead you back to safe and sane places.

A Give-Away

Pots of boiled beef in the pick-up truck,
Sweet corn, frybread and pies,
Piles of hand sewn quilts and star pillows,
Dancing shawls, bright cloth and scarves,
Sister is having a give-away.

New grass ripples under black beetles,
Crocus and lilacs inhale the sky,
Young cottonwoods talk in the breeze,
Whirlwind scatters the quail,
Earth is having a give-away.

Uncle laid the feathers side by side,
Eagle, Hawk, Owl and Mallard,
Guests all to this man's prayers,
Sacrificed for honor, love, ancient promises,
Ceremony is having a give-away.

Drunks greet each other out around back,
Liquor store hasn't opened yet,
Acapulco gold floats from abandoned cars,
Teenagers are sending smoke signals,
The pitiful are having a give-away.

A young girl planned solitude for 3 weeks,
Her spring was a rape in the cornfield,
Distance so quiet, no one heard her prayers,
.30-.30 rifle scattered her shame in the outhouse,
Life is having a give-away.

A Present-Day Creation Story

Waking next to you, I see a soul on the verge
of flesh. A pulse strong, but wavering takes
residence on your throat. Mist gathers above a
mouth wanting to utter faithful dialogues.

Your arms at peace, rest quietly across a chest
surging with hope. But I know when you wake,
vows will disappear into the light. Your voice
and walk will make way for aged enemy habits.

I bargain to enter creation's gate, give my word
to uphold growth and sight, don primordial skin,
throw away my mind and travel back to when
pipestone was clay. Salamander hearing my

urgent flight, crawled out of liquid night, blinked
at this half-crazed woman and whispered
instructions for regenerating a heart. Referred
to a nearby creek, I witness blue turn red and

watch the blood spread, shaping mud into the
likeness of reptiles and men. A dancing terrain
called me to hear earth chanting new traveling
songs for your birth — granite and lava shifting

in her womb. West wind blowing through us
cast our voices louder, splintering rock into silver
bones. Salamander eyeing coming fire, extended
his fingers to the east and invited dawn to clothe

the skeletal creation. Only the grandfathers
know how the stars contributed to your soul. And,
of all the souls that reach and leave, yours chose
to stay for the noble event — to unify with earth,

and to rest now and then. All year your widening
circle lured me to this point. Your tongue, void
of sound, hurries to leave silence. Subtracted of
movement, I see you wanting to take custody of

bones and flesh. While you slept, I had become
a mirror — caught a reflection you had set aside.
Now dreaming under your restless arms, I wonder
when to impart these beliefs, and with morning

leaning into our space, I struggle with the urge
to hold on to salamander's night. I touch the
red stone in my deer skin heart and pull your
sleeping breath closer to the healing side.

As you stir, I close my vision and narrate back
to now. "This is a present day creation story,
your walk will gain spirit each time you wake."

All He Hoped There Would Be

It was after the celebrating, when drink dulled
their energy and called for a space to resign
attitude and body. Couples from the high plains
and southern flats drifted into rooms within rooms,
looking to find an all night ceremony. Talk was
attempted until the last round was enough to put
them down. They whispered the need to hold on
like they knew there were more places to fall.

I've been in a poem like this before, watching an
Indian man not wanting to risk taking an Indian
woman sober. Heart scarred long ago by the
leaving of the first woman. Trust also left that time,
easier now waking up the morning after, with the
catch of the of the night, his indulgence his excuse,
pretending for the rest of his days what never was,
what his mother's leaving never did to him.

Maybe this isn't that man. Maybe he's one of those
wild four legged who needs other wild things, savors
the chase at his pace, the urge to move in and on,
his rhythm slow and steady, keeping up with the
animal of his dreams, heart beating against her back,
like hooves beating the land, horse dancing so many
times for pleasure, it happens even in sleep. But that
was another poem . . . .

He knows of the kind who lives only for the now,
like the warriors of long ago who truly lived for each
day. That's when women and men shared their visions,
when both knew what to do with the knowledge. Back
then spirits knew spirits, nothing had to be explained.
Foremost was trust, not taking a risk, and every day
was a good day to die. He wished he was that life,
living in verse, gaining the night.

His woman slowly closed her eyes and heard him call
out someone else's name, but she held his head, lost
between her shoulder and the leaving of the other woman.
Her state of mind overtook them both, her breathing in,
him breathing out. His presence? A state of believing,
where his essence was slipping minute by minute into
every quiet space of her being, naming in his woman,
all he ever hoped there would be.

Cousins, You Remind Me

Memories hold quiet thoughts this hour of
warm Chelsea days, blinding sun scorching
the flat, the sagebrush, and the stones while
hundreds of meadowlarks sang our songs.
Our retreat was kept cool by the waving
arms of chokecherry where we cousins
would expand creative doors for our play.

Cousin, you remind me of the words our
grandfather lived by. He was a judge,
living on two roads — choosing the best
for the people, and dedicated to making an
offering for all the children. We all wanted
to live the same way — principled and
loving toward all. You too choose the
sacred tree and loved all God's children.

Cousin, I remember your voice, a breath on
cold Christmas nights, brought peace and
joy in duet and Dakota. Neighbors peered
out to listen and share a knowing smile.
How we were raised was the message. There is
no silence in heaven when souls become songs
to drift with stars along the milky way.

Thank you cousins, I remember in our day
how we arranged our lives around the wants
and needs of our siblings. Then in later years
it was in service to our children. At times when
we grew tired, we sat in the tall grass under
cottonwoods, lingered among willows along
the coulee or lost ourselves with June berries
where angels eased weary brows and hands.

My relatives, you worked hard, but you knew
that peace was found in giving. You gave your
heart, your time, your soul. During the "Moon of
Falling Leaves" and during the "Moon When Deer
Lose Their Horns" your earthly lives were called back
To the Spirit Road. Now, memories will hold me close.
My cousins, you will always remind me.

Notes:

Moon of Falling Leaves is the month of October.
Moon When Deer Lose Their Horns is the month of November.

Masks

Masks carve deep, beyond nerve and bone,
chip through stone and reason, implore
pretense to fall away. It is midnight and I beg
this dark image layered and cold take leave
for now. In nighttime prayers, culture opens
a door of reprieve till wounds are examined,
and healed, till needs are satisfied. I turn you
into legend, share poised truths with your coyote.

Ask me if I know the wildness and survival of
the mystic dog, the playfulness and pretense of
their strange games. I watch your coyote — hooked
on enemy's scent, trickle motive for appetite,
track other habitat for sport, pace breath until
the kill, until all need is fed. Filling up and
instinct become your body — your diligent work.
Some called it greed; others called it survival.

Coyote spirit howling and pointing watches us under
a laughing moon as we chase each other in circles,
while we wonder who in this hell cast our shadows
like this on grandmother earth. When you became
coyote, you transformed native essence into a hairy
form and took up hunger to get you through lasting
nights of fevers and flight, through forced long walks,
through crushed promises and ultimate trail's end.

Each time I look at you I see disquieted hope, always
one final breath. From this I shake diamond back's
tail, backtrack my horses. Listen, these trying times
were only for a season, one of our past lives. All this
glares from under your mask, lacerates moments for
me, bleeds out in your quiet voice, a voice I've heard in
former lifetimes. Your fever has broken, your flesh is
now rebuilding. Come, I too have mingled in masks.

Building a Fire

We all have our own way of building a fire.
We start with dried grasses, carefully pile on
Cottonwood kindling, point the small branch
Tips toward the center, and lay slow burning
Logs on top. We rub stone against flint, spark a
Light, blow on the embers, urge out small flames.

We watch red energy leap into life, dark faces
Glow, eyes reflect a drum, everyone sings, is
Happy. We become one as we reach for warmth,
For our stories. Unattended the fire could go out,
So we prepared, we lit tobacco, in ceremony we
Gave clay pots of coals to all the clans, promised
To keep seven campfires burning forever, forever.

We never thought our fires would be smothered,
Never dreamed how quiet the night, but there were
Visions of a dawn with no light, elderly faces with
No eyes or mouths, our children seen with spotted
Bodies, woke up confused. We found our parents
Dead — no one to greet the day. Then our fires
Began to go out — one by one. We prayed, but
No answer. We thought our Gods had also died.

In searching, we stumbled upon one small twig gently
Smoldering, remembered dried sweet grass, found our
Spirits along the way, heard our words turn into new
Songs. That raging light in the east took pity on us,
Lent courage to our ashes, wind danced for our coals,
Broken limbs began to gather from distant woods,
And once again, in abundance, we flared and roared.

This is one of the stories we will tell. We'll always
Remember sound without the crackle of flame, time
Without wisdom of the old ones. And, with stronger
Tendered, red voices, we will show our children how
To dream again, to sing, to pray, to tend to the last coal.
We'll tell of the time fire taught us to build our lives
So we would never die out.

Welcome the Wakinyan

It was during the moon when the rains came.
Water flowed down my windows, my street, over
my feet, the land. I smelled the coming of
bulging rivers, felt the dampness moving, then
I heard the running, when everything took cover.

A dark form stirred, shadowy, feathered wings
stretched. Branches creaked. Birds hid. Air was
forced aside. Flight was with determined effort.
Light exploded as Wakinyan lifted and swirled
into the dangerous darkness above called home.

Thunder, that ancient cry, freed from the sky
traveled through my hair, my skin, struck
my memory. I saw foreboding, nest-like
clouds form and shift, like a unity of ions, then
come together to welcome the Wakinyan.

Vibrating with pressure, wanting to purify all life,
black and graying mist transformed into millions of
raindrops, bursting with a roar. Leaves and buds
were flattened. Wakinyan commanded and led the
cleansing of earth and other beating hearts.

On the low windy plain a four-legged stomped
four times, saluted all directions. His black
mane whispered, "It is time to escort the rain."
Shoulders worked, nostrils flared and flanks
stretched as Sunka Wakan galloped into the west.

If you fire up sweet grass, point a sacred pipe
toward the darkening sky, offer food, the clouds
will part and pass you by. But some forget,
forget to honor the earth and the Gods above.
They forget to tell the ancient stories.

And it is they who will see the feathered one
flash glaring eyes and watch lightning turn to fiery
leashes. It is they who become captive to the warning
sound, become slaves to the all knowing light, and
are forever driven ahead of the thundering hoof beats.

Notes:

Wakinyan is the thunderbird.
Sunka Wakan is the horse.

Chandi for Little Buddy

Did you hear the sirens early this morning?
she asked as I answered the phone. None
were heard in this part of town, but she was
insistent that they rang for several minutes.

She was anxious to say that Anderson's old
abandoned trailer house had burned down.
She said it was Little Buddy. I had just left
the local market and was driving down

Highway 2 back to my house. I just saw
Little Buddy outside the casino sharing a
story with the street people and counting his
money. He wasn't little, about 6 feet 4 and

250 pounds. A gentle soul who opted for
Viet Nam rather than a life of alcoholism.
He left 'Nam' wounded from napalm fire
and a habit for all the smoke, needles and pills

one could imagine. When he saw me he
asked for my spare change, said he was
heading east and wanted to buy some chandi.
He followed me to the car, but I told him I

needed my own money. As I got into my car
I heard him say, "That's okay cousin, just
wanted to say hello." My sister figured that
Little Buddy was probably smoking and then fell

asleep. That old trailer was a death trap, she said. I was thinking that Little Buddy wasn't so persistent like he usually was, just a big grin on his face. Later my sister called and

said Little Buddy died in that trailer some time before, probably from too much drink, then passed on from asphyxiation. He had been missing for a couple of days. Sometimes

those gentle hearts show their true light when it's their time. After a lifetime of living with fire he made his way downtown to say goodbye before heading east. Later that day, sister and I

offered up some chandi for Little Buddy.

Note:

Chandi is tobacco.

IV. Iwahoiciya (We Promise)

They Still See Us

We have lived on numerous levels of past lives.
The Grandfathers and Grandmothers have led us
safely through cleansing waters, through centuries
of underground paths, from angels to neutrinos,
from buffalo lives to the present common man,
and we are still not done with this earth walking.
The eternal Grandfathers and Grandmothers still
see us walking holy, still see us living the way of
the four directions. And, one day, they will see
us continuing toward the milky way.

Cante T'inswaya Manipelo

(for my father)

Man being walking the earth in red paint
spirit armed with belonging and recount.
Your shield, a male elk, with the endorsement
of the spirit that causes everything to move,
talk to us in behalf of the stars from where
you came. This plain is dusty and dry, we
have come to a fork in the blood, where
choice is a new beginning. Every dawn this
century we have looked for that thunder that
was ours. You have walked like a daring
warrior across our site, a vision we want
to make our own. We hear the wind from
the third direction, help us explain it to the
children, that place where clouds carry the
seeds of their name. The yesterdays of the last
era have been the same for the lightning and
the rain, bringing us renewing rivers every
season, yet we decline away from the song
of nature, our ancient ancestor, the voice of
the horse's windy cry. You have lain asleep,
unafraid wherever you walk. So you lived.
Now you tell us to live that way and take
courage. Challenge us about our relationship
to all that is. We were led away from
believing we were born of earth and spirit,
but we were cast to attend to all of earth's
beings, to sing prayers of adoration for her
offspring. You teach us that only then can we
attach to our hair the feather of the intrepid hawk.
You tell us we must dream ourselves to whole
humans and walk this place, not in this world
of another's making, but side by side with the
entity that gives breath and makes all things move.

Notes:

Cante t'inswaya Manipelo means "They walk courageously."
That which "makes all things move" is called Daku Skan Skan.

A Song for the Red Tipi Children

This time you will be raised in the sun
Come Red Tipi Children
Sacred Children of Wakan Tanka

This time you will be safe and loved
In the sanctuary of the Red Tipi
Sacred Children of Wakan Tanka

This day songs were created for you all
Children in the arms of the Red Tipi
Sacred Children of Wakan Tanka

This is the time for healing and living
Red Tipi will see you to a new day
Sacred Children of Wakan Tanka

Note:

The Red Tipi was considered sanctuary for any and all who were needing protection. It was usually set up for families and individuals who were escaping warring tribes. Today we see our own children needing sanctuary from society's ills.

Making Things Straight

> He was always running around with a hammer trying to flatten round and curvy things (soup bowls, eggs, wagon wheels, etc.), thus making them straight. (Describing a thunder dreamer)
> — John Fire Lame Deer

Auntie was never afraid of thunder. Born during a storm,
she knew her early beginnings, knew the passion of forces
that brought her to this living. And, it was her concern for
all her children that kept her going. In her Santee tongue
it was hers, her sister's, and her female survivors
that brought her to care for the energy that surrounded them.
Always mindful of their dreams and revelations,
she encouraged talk and closeness. It was that one day
when the thunder and lightning would not stop
that she shared her power. As the western disturbance
moved upon the family home, the shriek
of thunder birds grew louder, the flashes of light illuminated
every shiny thing in the house till sparks darted in and out the windows.
All the children huddled in one big chair hoping
for safety in the cushions. Auntie putting her foot down,
advanced to the kitchen where we heard her hacking and pounding
on what we would soon find out. She threw open the front door
and out she went into the storm. Outside in the rage of light
her silhouette was one of respect as she offered
the storm a choice cut of deer back strap. She hoisted the meat
onto the roof and cried out a plea, "Take this, the best of what I have,
and leave my children back to their quiet and peaceful dreaming."
The storm left immediately.

Not Just Heard, but Practiced

Used to be that bravery was taught
to the children every day.
Used to be that bravery was urged
among the children every day.
Used to be that bravery was shown
to the children every day.
Used to be that bravery was practiced
for the children every day.

Taught by the old in everyday games.
Shown by the old in everyday decisions.
Advised by the old in everyday stories.
Practiced by the old in everyday rules.

Bravery is not just heard, but practiced.

Bravery is a way of being.
Bravery is a way of doing.
Bravery is a way of living.
Bravery is a way of speaking.

Walk over here young person.
Stand next to me young person.
Sit down by me young person.
Listen to me young person.

I will show you a game of conviction.
I will practice the decision I make.
I will tell you a story of survival.
I will advise you on rules to live by.

We exist because we love our ways.
We do good to receive from earth.
We live our lives for the children.
We speak of our love for the spirit.

Bravery is practiced.

We Will Listen

We will listen to the pulse of your skin
  as it sinks and floats protecting your heart.
We will praise all your beautiful dreams,
  because hope is alive and will not depart.

We will listen to the voice you have hidden
  as all your words are meant to be known.
We will praise all the songs you want to sing,
  because angels have said you will be shown.

We will listen to the person you want to be
  as your spirit and your energy is returning.
We will shout praises as courage is restored,
  because faith heals all and is now emerging.

We will listen to all your once silent days
  as tears dry and all your prayers are safe.
We will shout praises as you learn of trust,
  because God's love is so full of grace.

The Way the Rain Came

Çepaśi, this season, let us walk the
way the rain came, unexpected but
always welcome. "Come in, come in,
sit and visit a while," my auntie would
say as she wiped the kitchen table and
laid out a fresh loaf of bread. "This
year we've had a lot of rain," she said.
"Thunder so loud it killed the spiders."
That's what she always says. The rain
and cold sent all the bugs and spiders
into her house. She sent them to the
other world then blamed the thunder.
Every day for a whole week a fine lined
mist enveloped the houses. "When you
come, you make me happy," she laughed.
"I feel like a flower that's been watered."
Her smile so large it made her eyes close.
She said she has ancestral roots that have
been buried deep under her house for a
long, long time. Her leaves were her
bread, her flower was her Dakota voice.
"If it's windy, be sure and shut the door;
if it's warm, leave it open, but don't come
if you have to leave right away." Now
every time it rains, in memory of Auntie,
all I can do is stand in her shadow and
walk the way the rain came.

Note: Çepaśi is a female cousin.

Dancing with Deer

(for Elaine)

Here we are, sister, sitting in our finest deerskin
dresses, waiting for the dance to begin. Deer

would hold their heads high upon viewing what
finery their sacrifice has created. I fixate my

eyes and visit with a four-legged, not imaginary,
but an invited spirit. I see her coming across

the arena a stately being, rounded back and
firm thighs, a pleasing gait, oval eyes, large,

innocent, beckoning hypnotic attention to
her style. I hear the whistle of a lone song

coming deep from strong red voices inhaled
during dawn breezes and exhaled from lungs

forceful as earth's rotations. I understand her
power, the kind that fills air with prophetic

dreams and grandma's legendary tales of
pairing with man, the promise only the gift

giving can convey. I feel a motion beginning
in sinew born of tinted bark and energy of

seasonal poplar growth, a step tethered with
vine for each new moon. As she nears, her

scent sends me to prairies of sage, where
rivers lead me to sweet grass and gardens of

warrior's flowering tobacco for my pouch of
charms, sachet and smoke. Come sister, the

drummers are singing our favorite song,
tonight we are dancing with deer.

Maka Odowa

Sitting on the back porch this morning
tiny footsteps hurried through my prayer,
I opened my eyes to the scurry of a field
mouse. It paused, picked up an offering of
grasses, begged to exchange prayers with
me, then hopped off in the sparse morning
breeze drifting through narrow fence spaces.
A dove poised gently on the arc of dawn
appealed for attention to its solitary voice.
I strained to find its direction, to listen one
more time, waiting for clarification, but only
an echo. A slash of warmth crossed my face
from the space I had leaned into. The sun
was making its way over the roof. Quickly I
leaned back into the comfort of my chair, into
the cool quiet of eaves and thick tree trunks.
All of a sudden the wind, an octave higher,
signaled the rattle of poplar leaves into a
crescendo of near escape from their stems.
Then as suddenly, the choir was slowed into
a hushed liturgy. In another kind of ritual, a
dragonfly maneuvering over the rose bush,
secretly kissed each pink rose hip with its
delicate hands. Its hum was like the exhale of
a baby's breath, its wings reflected the DNA
of crystal and conch shell. Again the breeze
with messages from some far off wheat field,
sang in praise of harvest. I had gone out to
pray, thought to author another early morning
invocation. Instead, this day, my grandmother
claimed ownership with her eternal earth song.

Notes:

Maka – earth
Odowa - song

Tell Me

Tell me the pulse guiding my skin
Sinks and floats to protect my heart.
Tell me my dreams are all very real,
That hope is alive and will never depart.

Teach me the tongue of ancestor times
I want a language I can speak today.
Teach me songs that please the children
A voice lifting in celestial array.

Thank me for the lives you spent with me
Where night exhaled the essence of you.
Thank me when vision starts to be true
United souls, known only by a few.

Take me to your morning star
Where early rising is a godly task
Take me to where prayers are now safe
Eternity a blessing, we just have to ask.

Trespassing in English

Told you were wicistinma (sleeping), a dormant form
just now giving up your hibernation. Wetu (Spring)
started without you. Mahpiya (a cloud) squeezed rain
over your roof and hurried past that West Coast
hanyetuwi (moon). Inside your humble tipi (home),
a television announcer exchanges and bargains in English —
a solid drone of wasicu (white) noise encroaching on
your canku (path) to dreaming in Dakota (Sioux). I hear
your partner try to wake you, "You're wanted" (on the
phone). "They need you," (to pick up), words traveling
through veins of another kind, rushing along Highway 2,
across tin'ta (the prairie) at the speed of light into the
receiving end of my waiting makamibe (world). Inside
my receiver that local train, switching through your
otonwahe (town or village) is heard in Montana. It
breaks a short whistle (short of me hanging up). I place
myself in your taku o'ksan un (environment), see an
uneasy pose, blinking at the waiting anpetuwi (sun),
head hanging off the edge (of the bed). An extremity
flinches like you trying to stop a fall, or you taking flight —
a late rendezvous with muscles trying to let go (of sleep),
then giving in to waking (in English). You open your
eyes, wonder why it's wikawankap'u (around seven or
eight a.m.), wonder who is calling so early? It is just your
koda (friend) and spring in kicieconpi (competition) with
the TV, that train, trespassing your space in English.

Picking Plums North of the Pow-Wow Grounds

Here, wet earth pulses waves of cool
air over my feet, touching warm skin
then catching my breath with fresh
summer growth. Afternoon sun done,
but lingering, shines on this isolated
grove surrounded by willow, sage, and
chokecherry. I reach for branches heavy
with plums and touch the ripeness of
pink fruit. Gnats and mosquitoes race
my fingers through fragrant leaves and
form tiny circles of flight around eager
hands. I pluck and pull. My pockets
and jacket hood bulge with plums.
Juice runs down my chin, my arms, and
slowly colors my clothes. Sweetness
fills the air, my hair, and my senses.
In a sudden awareness I realize my
driving frenzy and pause. Up against the
nearby hills — hues of pine and pink dust
scatter across red rock and new grasses —
horses grazing raise their heads to watch
as I obtrusively make my way through
the plum patch. I nearly missed the
grace of sorrels and pintos who have
always received from this land just
north of the powwow grounds.

Porcupine on the Highway

Amos: They said sister is stranded on the highway.
Her car is about 10 miles east of town.
Sister: I might as well pick up this porcupine or
it'll be smashed by tonight.
Porcupine: I give my body to a quill worker,
and laugh at Magpie on the fence.

Amos: Mom, I'm taking Myrna to help sister.
Her car quit and I might have to tow her in.
Sister: Oh, it's a big one and the quills
aren't damaged. It's got long hair, too.
Porcupine: Clouds are fading. Earth is cooling.
Grass is calling me home.

Amos: There she is. She put something in her trunk.
It looks like a big old porcupine.
Sister: This sure is a mess. I should skin it here.
All the cats will be coming into the yard.
Porcupine: They used to read my bones, study my
entrails for health and weather.

Amos: What happened? Did you break down?
Don't tell me, you're scavenging road kill?
Sister: Yeh, both! All of a sudden this thing
stalled, then I saw this huge porcupine.
Porcupine: They say our voice sounds like a
whimpering child. People gather.

Amos: Pull your hood latch. Your cable was loose.
Take it home and skin it. We'll follow you.
Sister: I'll make Myrna a quilled bracelet and
brother some armbands. Surprise them.
Porcupine: She'll remember later that last week she
dreamed about a big porcupine on the highway.

Note:
U.S. Highway 2, eastern Montana between Wolf Point and Poplar.

Wicoiye Waśte
ka Woeye
Favorite Dakota/Lakota (Sioux) Words and Phrases

Tatanka Iyotaka — Sitting Bull, Medicine man of the Hunkpapa Sioux.
Ta Oyate Duta — His Red People, Chief of the Santee Sioux .
Si Tanka — Big Foot, Chief of the Hunkpapa who was killed in the massacre under a white flag at Cankpe Opi Wakpala (Wounded Knee Creek), South Dakota with 390 of his followers on December 29, 1890.
Kagi Yatapi — Crow King, Hunkpapa war chief, led 80 warriors in Battle of Little Big Horn enabling Crazy Horse and Gall to succeed in their attack on Custer.
TaSunka Witko — His Horse is Spirited (Crazy Horse), Oglala War Chief.
Pezi — Gall, Hunkpapa (Lakota) War Chief.
Hehaka Sapa — Black Elk, Lakota Spiritual Leader.
Inkpa Duta — Scarlet Point, Santee Sioux Chief.
Wanata — He Who Charges, Chief of the "Cuthead" Yanktonai who led 1,300 wariors.
Mahpiya Luta — Red Cloud, Head War Leader and Chief of the Oglala Sioux.
Sinte Gleska — Spotted Tail, Brule Lakota Tribal Chief.
Wizikute — Pine Shooter, Chief of the Yankton Sioux.
Wakan Tanka — Greatest Universal Spiritual Power (God).
Maka Ina/Unci — Grandmother/Mother Earth's two aspects: birth and wisdom.
He Sapa — Black Mountains (Black Hills). Sacred place to many tribes.
Pte Oyate — Buffalo Nation (Ancestors, who we were before coming to the surface).
Ikceya Oyate — Common man (What we are now).
Canku Duta — The Red Road, the sacred road the Sioux follow to the Great Spirit.
Canku Sapa — The Black Road, the road of war and strife.
Candeska Wakan — Sacred Hoop, medicine wheel, sacred way of life.
Mitakuye Oyasin — All My Relations, includes plant, animals, earth, all elements.
Hococa — Camp circle.
Tamakoce Tehindapi — Patriot.
Itanca — Leader.
Wakincoza — Elder or respected one who located, led, and arbitrated camp issues.
Wotihnisa — Hunter, took care of family, relatives, and elders.
Tiwahe — Household, immediate family.
Omawahiton — In-laws.
Winyan — Woman.

Wicasta — Man.
Tukasila — Grandfather.
Unci — Grandmother.
Wakan Yeza — Sacred being (a baby).
Wapostan — Cradle board.
Winona — Oldest daughter.
Wakasotesni — Female virgin.
Wimnasni — Male virgin.
Caske — Oldest son.
Koda — Friend, not a casual remark, means a friend for life.
Dakota — The Eastern Sioux (Isanti or Santee) using the "D" dialect. Means allies.
Lakota — The Western Sioux (Teton) using the "L" dialect. Means allies.
Pabaksa — Cut Head band of Yankton Sioux. (Decapitated their enemies.)
Hunkpapa — End of Horn. (People who camp by themselves.)
Isanti — By The Knife. (Original band of Sioux Nation.)
Kaposia — Light Weight (A band of Sioux known to travel light.)
Wamakaskan — Moving beings of the earth (animals).
Tatanka — Buffalo, reminder of greater whole.
Wanbdi/ Wanbli — Eagle, ruler of the sky on which we send prayer.
Sungmanitu/ Sungtokeca — Wolf.
Sunka — Dog, companion.
Sunka Wakan — Horse (Spirit Dog).
Sunktahuwasaka — Strong Necked Horse.
Sunonk'onpa — Dog or horse drag (travois).
Mato — Bear, represents medicine.
Mastincana — The Rabbit, represents humility.
Cetan — Hawk, fast, fearless, on target.
Tahca — Deer, animal of legends and gifts.
Sinte sapela — Black Tailed Deer.
Ista dopa — Four Eyes (name describes a dog with brown spots above its eyes).
Sintehda — Rattlesnake (tail rattles).
Iktomi — Spider (also the trickster).
Tusweca — Dragonfly, represents speed and spirit of whirlwind.
Kimimina — Butterfly, represents joy.
Unhcegila — Mastodon.
Mniwasicu — Water Spirit, guardian of the water.
Tipi — Tent.

Akicita — Warrior Police.
Wapa Yusdoha — War Bonnet.
Bdota hunka — War Chief.
Caksa — War Club.
Iyakisa — War Cry.
Ozuye — War Party.
Wicoha — War Deed.
Tokala — Kit Fox (society) upheld ideals of generosity and honor.
Ska Yuha — White Owner (white horse owner).
Tatanka Wapahun — Buffalo Headdress Society.
Wotawe — The personal consecrated armor, a war medicine bundle.
Iyakapemni — War weapon.
Wase Wakan — Sacred red protective paint.
Iyok'iheya kte — Following the Killing (counting coup).
Winyan Nunpapi — Double Woman. Dream woman who brought the art of quill work to the Sioux.
Heyoka — A thunder dreamer, contrary or a anti-natural god.
Heyoka ti — The place where the Heyoka does his wakan (sacred) work.
Winkte — Woman-like man (Two Spirits). They are highly regarded.
Yumni — God of games.
Whope — Falling Star.
Inyan — The Rocks.
Peta — The Fire.
Pejin wacipi — Grass dance.
Kahomni — Turn about (dance).
Nasdoha Wacipi — Dragging foot (round dance).
Iwakici Wacipi — Dance in Praise of One (Victory dance).
Wiconi — Good life as a human being.
Maka Wiconi — The sacred life on earth.
Daku Skan Skan — That which makes everything move.
Wanagi-tacanku — Spirit Road or Milky Way.
Wahakiktapi — Wake (stay awake all night).
Wokiksuye Kicagape — Memorial feast.
Ituh'anpi — A formal give-away.
Wicoozi Makoce — Happy Hunting Ground (afterlife).
Wiyo ate — Father Sun.
Anpo Wicahpi — Dawn (morning) Star.
Bdoketu — Potato time (Summer).

Ptayetu — Turn over time (Autumn).
Waniyetu — Breath (Winter).
Wetu — Sap or blood (Spring).
Anpetu — Daylight.
Wihinapa — Sunrise (Sun comes into lodge).
Anpo — Light (dawn).
Hihanna — It arrives (morning).
Wiwankatuya — About nine o'clock in the morning.
Wicokanhiya-sam-iyaye — Sun comes to middle, goes past (noon).
Wiyaspa — Bitten off moon (half moon).
Wimahiyaya — Sun goes into (sunset).
Anpa wiwante — A sun died (a complete solar eclipse).
Hanhepi wi — Moon (night sun) Shade, shadow.
Htayetu — Dim (dusk).
Hanyetu — Night, covering (evening).
Hancokan — Middle, center, night (midnight).
Wicahpi — Star.
Wicahpiha — Clear, starlit night.
Wioheyanpata — East direction, Eagle, prayer.
Itokagatakiya — South direction, Wolf, compassion.
Wiohpeyatakiya — West direction, Bear, medicine.
Waziyatakiya — North direction, Buffalo, wisdom.
Sinkpe tawota — Muskrat food (the medicine Sweet Flag).
Mato Pejuta — Bear Medicine (the medicine called Osha).
Winawizi — Jealous Woman (describing the burrs of the licorice plant).
Ceyaka — Dakota mint tea.
Wasna — Pemmican.
Tiyospaye — Family and extended family.
Oceti Sakowin — Seven Council Fires.
- Mdewakantonwan — People of Spirit Lake, Dakota.
- Wahpekute — Leaf Shooters, Dakota.
- Wahpetonwan — People of the Leaves, Dakota.
- Sissitonwan — People of the Swamp, Dakota.
- Ihanktonwan — Village at the End, Dakota.
- Ihanktonwanna — Little Village at the End, Dakota.
- Tetonwan — People of the Prairie, Lakota.

Wakakans'a — Story Teller.
Ohunkankan Ehankehanni — Ancient incredulous stories told.

Ohukakan — Stories of the domain of the supernatural.
Wicooyake — Stories of the domain of man.
Wicahmunga — Wizard.
Winyan Wicahmunga — Witch.
Can otipi — Dwell in the trees (little people).
Pte incala skawin — White Buffalo Calf Woman.
Hunka Lowanpi — Ceremony where one person adopts another as a relative.
Isnati Awicalowan — To live alone (girl's puberty ritual).
Tape Wankayeyapi — Throwing of the ball.
Wanagi Yuhapi — Ghost keeping.
Hable/habde ceya — Crying for a vision (vision quest).
Inipi — Sweat Lodge, where all is represented, the fire represents God.
Wiwayan Wacipi — Dance looking at the sun (Sun Dance).
Wakan Wicohan — Sacred Acts, deeds, ways.
Cancega — Drum.
Cancega mimela — hand drum.
Odowan — Song.
Cot'anka — Flute, Wiikizo siyotanka.
Ya'usiyaked — Speak humbly when admonishing a child.
Wicincana wan icimani — A little girl traveler has arrived (newborn girl).
Tanyan yahi — Glad you came (Welcome).
Taku tokha he? — What is going on?
Tokeske yaun he? or Toked yaun he? — How are you?
Tehan wancinyanke sni! — Long time no see!
De/Le mazaska tona he? — How much is this?
Taku ca yacin he? — What do you want?
Anpetu waste yuha — Have a nice day.
Tanyan omani — Good walking (Bon voyage).
Toksa ake — Later again (departing wish).
Anpetu waste yuha — Have a nice day.
Pidamaya — Thank you.
Nape mayuza — Shake my hand (extend hand in friendship).
Iyomakpi — I'm happy.
Inajin — Stand up.
Iyotanka — Sit down.
Hiyu — Come here.
Iyaye — Go.
Iho wana! — Now! (A signal to start.)

Inahni! — Hurry up!
Ahasisi! — Be careful!
Kikta! — Wake up!
Wanituka he? — Are you tired?
Istinma — Sleep.
Iwanka — Go to bed.
Nayah'un — Do you hear?
Tanyan istinma — Good night.
Wateca — Left overs.
Wacinksapa — Be attentive. (A reminder that God is continually present.)
Daku ni caze? — What is your name?
Mitakuyepi Lois Red Elk emaciyape naha iyuha cante wasteya nape ciyuzape. — I am called Lois Red Elk and, my relatives, I shake your hands with good feelings in my heart.
Demakota. — I am a Dakota.
Montana hemataha. — I come from Montana.
Billings hedwati. — I live in Billings.
Mi kunsi cante waste yuha. — My grandmother has a good heart.
Mahpiya Luta, Lakotamayasi na. — Red Cloud, you told me to be an Indian.
Tatanka ska he wakan. — The white buffalo is sacred.
Anpo kun hehan sungtokeca ki ho. — The coyote howled at dawn.
Anpetu de cante mi waste. — This day my heart is good.
Cante ed yuza / Iyotancila. — Love you.
Ki Iyanka Okancu — A sacred circular track around the Black Hills.
Wikiake eceti — The sun built a fire around self (sun-dogs).
Mazaska — White iron (money) silver dollar.
Mazasksala —Red white iron (penny).
Koktopawage sakowin sam opawage sakowin sam wikcemna sakowin sam ake sakowin — 7,777 (seven thousands, more seven hundreds, more seven tens, again seven).
Kola, tuwa napeciha opaktesni ye — Friend, whomever flees shall not participate (song of the Strong Heart Society).
Canli/candi wapahte — Tobacco offering.
Canotida/canotila — Forest spirits (they live in a tree).
Iktomi tawokaske — Spider's strings (Spider's web).
Iya — The glutton, brother of Iktomi, who likes to eat people.
Lakol wicoh'an — The Lakota (Indian) way or spiritual way.
Pejuta winyela — A medicine woman. She uses herbs.

Tate — The wind, the father of the four winds.

Tunkasila ukiye — The Grandfathers are coming, meaning a storm is coming.

Wakinyan agli. — The thunder beings are coming.

Wakinyan etunwanpi. — The thunder beings are glaring (lightning).

Wakinyan hotunpi. — The thunder beings are talking (thunder).

Taku wakan mani — Something sacred walking.

Ho Tunkasila wakinyan niktepi. — Ho Grandfather, the thunder killed you.
(Expresion used when one accidentally kills a spider)

About The Author

Photo by Dennis Minawmish

Lois Red Elk is descended from the Isanti, Hunkpapa, and Ihanktowan bands of the Dakota/Lakota Sioux Nation. Her father, James Red Elk is a descendant of the Sitting Bull family, and her mother spoke five different languages, French, Latin, Sioux, Assiniboine and English. She enjoys writing poetry and prose and practices the art of porcupine quill embroidery. She has a Human Services Degree from Ft. Peck Community College and an Education Degree from Rocky Mountain College. Married to her dear friend and husband Dennis for 41 years, they have two children and eight grandchildren.